"When poetry is practical and applicable as balm to the soul, all tender places are strengthened and healed. Leonard A. Slade, Jr.'s poetry is a welcome salve to all of us who are in need."

—Dr. Maya Angelou
Reynolds Professor of American Studies
Wake Forest University

Lilacs in Spring

Book of Poems

Also by Leonard A. Slade, Jr.

Another Black Voice: A Different Drummer (1988)
The Beauty of Blackness (1989)
I Fly Like a Bird (1992)
The Whipping Song (1993)
Vintage (1995)
Fire Burning (1995)*
Pure Light (1996)*
Neglecting the Flowers (1997)*

**Available from McGraw-Hill*

Lilacs in Spring

Book of Poems

Leonard A. Slade, Jr.

The McGraw-Hill Companies, Inc.

New York St. Louis San Francisco Auckland Bogotá
Caracas Lisbon London Madrid Mexico Milan Montreal New Delhi
Paris San Juan Singapore Sydney Tokyo Toronto

McGraw-Hill
A Division of The ***McGraw-Hill*** *Companies*

Lilacs in Spring

1 2 3 4 5 6 7 8 9 0 BKM BKM 9 0 9 8

ISBN: 0-07-228900-7
Library of Congress Catalog Card Number 98-

Editor: M. A. Hollander
Cover Design: Maggie Lytle
Printer/Binder: Bookmart Press

For

Roberta Hall (my wife)
and
Minitria Elisabeth Slade (my daughter)

Table of Contents

Lilacs in Spring

He sucked a thumb in Kentucky,
where his father chopped wood
for warm evenings
in December. He wore old
clothes and walked barefoot
among lilacs in spring. And everywhere
he moved, Indiana and Illinois,
laughter filled the air

as young boys teased his height
and demeaned his clothes. No
child ever praised him,
and he for his suffering honored
her, all children thought small
of his future, except her
who read her *Bible* and loved him
as no other person could.

He studied by candlelight,
savoring words and defining dreams
for America. He was hungry for truth
and debated the pros and cons
of slavery. He promised a united country
but blood would taint freedom.
Brother against brother
sister against sister

blacks against whites
Northerners against Southerners—
they all fought for their cause.
Our father of freedom
bathed America with hope
and then was bathed himself
in cold blood.
Children cried.

I Came, I Saw, I Dreamed
(for Abraham Lincoln)

I see a child being born to save a country.
I see a spiritual giant being patient
    with a Southern belle.
I see a father grieving over the death of his child.
I hear cries and see tears showering the soul
    of a Nation.
I see parents sending their sons
    to fight for freedom.
I hear slaves praying and singing in the cotton fields.
I observe a U.S. President loved and hated,
    decisive and brave.
I see a country's savior, healing a people
    divided by war, slain by an assassin's bullet.
I see a country strong and powerful, beautiful and blessed.
I dream a better world.

Namecalling, with Love
(for Abraham Lincoln)

Abraham Lincoln:
Child
Man
Student
Husband
Father
Politician
Debater
Legislator
Builder
Dreamer

Agitator
Loser
Winner
Debtor
Believer
Thinker
Orator
Visionary
Giant
Spiritualist

Thank You, Abe!

Abraham Lincoln set me free,
Gave me dignity for the world to see.
Some have said he did not care
About my Blackness and the slavery affair.
But I sincerely and honestly believe
This man was called to help us breathe
Truth, righteousness, justice, and all.
America now stands proud and tall.
Thank you, Abe, for what you have done
For giving us victory that's almost won.

The Power of Love
(For President Abraham Lincolm)

You built your life in Kentucky, Indiana, and Illinois.
You studied *The Bible* for instruction and guidance.
Your study of law sharpened your debating skills.
You tickled one's intellect with your brilliant mind.
You were loved and despised nationwide.
But you held fast to high principles and enduring values.
You learned to absorb pain.
Your country depressed you,
Brother against brother,
Sister against sister.
Your family and your God sustained you.
You taught a people how to unite and triumph.
You taught the world the power of love.

Song for a Beautiful Lady
(for my wife)

Train rides and summer thoughts
weave a tune of joy and pleasure.

How often in life
can one witness such immense wealth
and Heavenly beauty?

The Great Being

Among animals
I like human beings in motion
jogging the highway
moving
rhythmically
determined to prolong
life
breathing relentlessly
mind alert
feet stretching
the steep mountain road ahead.

The Lombardy Poplar

The majestic poplar tree
taller than the house
last year produced
abundant beauty. But how
proud of limbs confronted
by wild winter winds?
Though strong it may be
there is no guarantee of long life.
Therefore water it often
and feed it with love
before the rites of spring.

What is a Mother?

She gives of her whole self.
She is an angel for the community.
She is the embodiment of spiritual love.

She knows her Bible
She practices what she teaches.
Her work speaks multitudes.

Her husband is her oneness.
Her children give her tears
That are heavenly showers to the soul.

May mothers find peace on earth
May heaven be their eternal Home.

The Brother
(Emmanuel Slade)

I have treasured
the brother
who reciprocated in
friendship

and who
loved unconditionally
giving of himself.

Bless him, Father,
he is something
so special
and so spiritual.

(26 February 1998)

A Friend

A friend should be gentle and kind
As an innocent child,
Sincere and seasoned
As the elderly ready for God.

President Karen R. Hitchcock

now President of
the University at Albany

of the State University
of New York

containing a microcosm of
a macrocosm

of higher education
changing the world

forever

(April 1998)

The Dean
(for Father William Small)

Inspiring.
Dynamic.
Intellectual.

He has the gift for preaching.
We listen. We recognize the power.
The power healing from God making us new
and lifting us to Heaven.

And in a short and fundamental period
a calling divine and pure
saved us.

He moved us—
who was a power,
who was a saint.

Dr. Maya Angelou

Brilliant. Beautiful.
Gracious. Grand.
Radiant. Rare.
She burns us with fire furious,
Sings us with pain and pleasure.
Her words are our power.
Her presence is our peace.
Her voice is our victory.
Eternity is her home.

Sergeant Henry Johnson

He believed in freedom
Fought for us,
Died in America's bosom.
He was black and beautiful,
Bold and the best
His heart was our love,
His beliefs were our future.
He gave us the world.
Selfless,
Visionary,
Spiritual.
His past was our history,
His dream was our present,
His life is in the Heavens.

Music on My Radio at 5 A.M.

Softly, by the fireplace, Bach is performing for me;
Taking me back to college days, when I was required
To listen to classical music on Saturday afternoons
And fulfill Music 101 requirements, taking notes on Mozart

And Beethoven at 5 A.M., the violin crying for love
And attention wakes Viotti from the grave, his heart now beats
To the old Saturday afternoon music in college, with snow outside
And notes in the air, the radio announcer my guide.

So now I wait for Handel to lift my soul
With the great arias of the past. The music
Of college days wakes me, my body is responding
In the depth of remembrance, I pray on my knees
  to be worthy today of this beauty and joy.

Mardi Gras at the Cathedral of All Saints

It's always like this:
an array of lights
splitting darkness,
colorful balloons
bursting joy,
a children's choir
sharing songs,
proud parents
strutting their stuff,
silent clowns
painting smiles,
saxophone players
doing their thing,
gumbo soup
scenting rooms,
cotton candy
ready to sweeten,
Angels in Heaven
ready to enter.

(February 1998)

Flying

Flying the skies
Is one way to dream
Of love and to celebrate
A smooth ride or
To adjust to bumps
Along the way
And to be reminded,
That's life.

(21 February 1998)

Sun, Moon, and Stars

Sunlight shines daily, now that spring is here.
Trees wear a coat of green leaves
and stand taller each day.
The red moon bleeds rays of romance
as never before known.

Stars twinkle nightly, smiling at darkness.
An owl hoots happily until midnight,
its sounds echoing the howling woods;
neighbors listen,
praying on their knees before bedtime.

Martha's Vineyard (Summer 1997)

Fitting our bicycle into the car,
Organizing our luggage around it
Gave birth to contentiousness
Between us,
But we pampered ourselves
On the road and
Forgave ourselves for the challenge
Of not being composed
Before separating from tense surroundings.
We learned somehow to greet the Ferry
With love before crossing the water
For Martha's Vineyard.
Seagulls glided above us
As we sat kissing the cool breeze
And laughing from the warm splashes
That tickled our faces.
Well, the end was near.
Vineyard Haven waved at us
As we walked to shore.
The taxi held our bicycle
In her steel arms
As we zipped through Oak Bluffs.
Once we reached the Harbor Inn in Edgartown
There was no turning back
For negative feelings.
We went to bed
And hugged the night
Losing ourselves in another world.

Oak Bluffs, Massachusetts

Please explain how Blacks and Whites
can travel together, dine together, wine
together, dance together, swim together,
play together, read together, stay together,
and pray together, in harmony, in Oak
Bluffs, Massachusetts, and yet others
cannot do the same in various regions
of the United States of America.

The Minister Said

To his music director
After Mass was over:
"Don't make me the son of a bitch
Because your assistant didn't excel today."
"You're in church," she said.

He walked away unremorseful.
Far away (in Hell) the devil was happy
Keeping his coals hot.

HAIKUS

"Steep Hill"

Running up the steep hill
his legs slowed down...
The downpour of rain

“Spring evening moon”

Spring evening moon;
a couple sitting by the ocean
kissing the breeze

"Fall beauty"

Fall beauty—
tall gold trees
regal and rich

"a black man"

a black man
emptying a trash can
in time for breakfast

“Summer flowers”

Cultivating the summer flowers
his caked hands hide blisters ...
The beauty of pain

"Blankets of snow"

Blankets of snow—
a child's dream realized
the day before Christmas

"Green Mountains"

Green Mountains—
scenic beauty caught
on a home video

"Black mother"

A black mother home alone
rocking her baby—
the thunderstorm

The Nursing Home

Such pain going through
the rooms of winter and

through a body, felt by elders.
Incoherence and screams make you humble

and your heart cries for rays of hope, but
don't worry there's not a group happier in

friendship and more giving in love. Joy
is a feeling we sometimes take for granted,

for old bodies can rest for hours, going
down private memory lanes. Listen,

the only way to accept homes nursing
is by seeing them firsthand, mind open

love
healing.

Don't Know Why

Sometimes I cry and don't know why,
Sometimes I laugh and almost die.
Then I cry and cry and cry.
Being Black is going to make me die.

A Stranger

I lived hundreds of miles from siblings.
Once a year I would travel to them,
The masks would hide bleeding hearts,
The children would study our whole being,
Fascinated by loud laughter communicating.
I would hug everybody present,
They would embrace me for various reasons.
Slowly I would wave goodbye again,
Make my departure uneventful until the next year.
In midyear I would travel to their city
Anxious, hoping responses to my Hyatt Regency
Invitation would celebrate, considering
That another year would pass before laughter belched.
As my twenty-four hour visit waited,
As the banquet halls watched for five siblings to enter,
I would stand for one tall brother to hug my greeting.
To look for others, to want love, to need
Togetherness with their physical presence,
Ourselves with each other, ourselves celebrating.
We would fail the connection
To support the presence of ourselves, to be together,
To come in peace, love, and joy.

I traveled back home a stranger.

The Daughter of My Best Friend

I once knew someone,
classically beautiful,
repugnant of big balls,
her body like Dorothy Dandridge,
hungry for love;
in spiritual harmony
she held her head high
and warmed females' lips;
out of the closet now,
in the public's eye,
alien to her family,
she struggled
like a slave
like a soldier
like a hero
to fight for her world.

Christmas Gift

Once a year
after feeding his fat pocketbook,
my father drives Mom from North Carolina
to Maryland, brags along the way about
how he reared his nine children in Jesus' Name,
prays fifteen minutes, hooping and hollering,
before each meal,
eats his children's steak and eggs,
and afterwards gathers around the Yule tree
to open his gifts.
He says, "It's the children's duty
to give my wife gifts. I
give her nothing."

The Preacher's Son

Such hatred flowing
through the veins and

into the soul, carried slowly
blackening the heart! Namecalling

and character assassination
became his pastime and the

community depended on him
for truth and righteousness.

There's nothing so terrible
as animosity. Love is

a feeling that Christians
have, and the soul can

struggle for years and
become a prisoner for sin. Look,

the preacher's old church
is burning to the ground

his son stands by gleeful
laughing like a pyromaniac

until a new church
is born.

Homage of My Ears

These ears are big ears
They hold secrets
Hear juicy gossip.
They are bigger than other ears.
Often they don't like what they hear.
These ears listen for knowledge.
They go where I go.
These ears are sensitive to sounds.
I have known them to hear words
That made me cry.

Black People

—whose ancestors suffered during the Middle Passage
To land in America filled with hopelessness,
Who lost the gift of freedom from Africa,
Each working in kitchens and fields,

Giants of strength and nobility
Whose hands and heads taught a country
Emancipation that fought racism,
Gave us will to make it, fight or die—

We bore freedom-fighter children,
Sacrificed our blood against hatred
Of cancerous oppression and stupid wars
Dying with dignity and proud

When with their hypocrisy and devilment,
The enemies seemed determined to destroy
Our minds and hearts that had the capability
To build a people. They battle us now in the '90's.

Poverty. Welfare. Affirmative Action. Prisons.
Crack babies. But we hold on.
We live on.
Defiant until the end of the world.

Facing the Future

American churches preach and teach Christianity;
Other religions have their own faiths.

Religious hypocrisy makes newcomers doubt
Evil priests and power-hungry members.

Once again, no singing. I wonder
If I could get preachers to pray

And without members hearing them.
I'll wait for ministers to clean the

Skeletons from their closets.
I, too, shall pray.

Sent to Question

Three hundred years, and more, have passed quickly.
Winter arrives annually with its snow and sleet.

I wonder before the beginning of spring: when
will I be free from my present depression and oppression?

The Country Club in the Academy

They were special:
Research scholars,
Published writers,
Politically correct professors.
They were elitist:
Ivy-League trained,
Holders of doctorates,
Intellectual snobs.
No way but the White way.
They were...now, now!
They are
Dead.

Monica and Bill

She entered the White House
Feminine and affectionate,
Becoming inebriated with power.
He trusted her smile
And accepted her hugs.
She loved his title
And needed his respect.
They are now at war
Lying, cheating, and destroying,
Relationships tainting
America's heart and soul.

Shooting at Westside Middle School, Jonesboro, Arkansas

He was now brokenhearted because
His thirteen-year-old girlfriend
Dropped him to be free for another.
She was loyal to her own principles
Concerning the rightness of having one
Boyfriend.
But he fought back with bullets
Killing a pregnant English teacher
And four innocent classmates.
His partner in crime assisted him.
Both now sit in a juvenile detention center
Guilty of killing any prospect for new love.
One requests pizza,
The other studies *The Bible.*
Is it now too late for Christ?

Boss Hogg

He enjoyed telling his members what to do
At church and in the community.
He loved being in charge, the head honcho,
Even when he was invited to family gatherings
He always found excuses for not coming.
He forgot all about the event, he said,
But the truth be known he wanted to
Emasculate my father, his deacon, publicly,
Control him, his mind and manner.
But independent thinkers cannot be slaves
And can make preachers miserable souls.
My father's convictions and values
Are rooted in *The Bible*.
No preacher can rule him.
Now I pray that my father and his preacher
Will not one day fight in Heaven.
God's angels will be reserving ringside seats.

Morning

Cocks crow. Clocks scream!
Darkness leaves the world.
Sunlight greets the day.
Eyes open. Bodies move.
Another good morning!

For You, America
(for Abraham Lincoln)

Come, I will make the country whole,
I will make the most beautiful rainbow of races ever known,
I will make diversity desirable in the workplace
            with the love of friends,
                        with the love of family.
I will plant the seeds of goodwill along the rivers
                        of America, and in the valleys, and
                        on every mountaintop,
I will make better my community by helping others,
                        By sharing,
                        By giving.
For you, America, I shall serve until death!
For you, for you, I am singing, hoping, loving, praying
For you!

Love

Nature —
animals
birds
flowers
rainbows
The sky.

Love
People —
children
parents
singles
gays
lesbians.

Love
The homeless
The hungry
The differently able
The oppressed.

Love
Truth
Justice
Mercy
Peace
Freedom.

Love
Love
Love.

Leonard A. Slade, Jr.

Leonard A. Slade, Jr., received the bachelor's degree in English from North Carolina's Elizabeth City State University, the master's degree in English from Virginia State University, and the Ph.D. degree in English from the University of Illinois at Urbana-Champaign. He taught for twenty-two years at Kentucky State University, where he was also Chair of the Division of Literature, Languages, and Philosophy, and Dean of the College of Arts and Sciences. In May 1989, Kentucky State University awarded him the Degree Doctor of Humane Letters. In May 1996, Elizabeth City State University awarded him a Doctor of Humane Letters degree. For several summers, he was writer-in-residence at Bennington College, Vermont, at The Bread Loaf Writers' Conference, Middlebury College, Vermont, and at The Ragdale Artists' Colony, Lake Forest, Illinois.

He has published in *Essence Magazine, U.S. News and World Report, The Courier-Journal, Ebony Magazine, The College Language Association Journal, The American Poetry Review, The Zora Neale Hurston Forum, The English Journal: Publication of the National Council of Teachers of English, The Journal of Southern History, The Black Scholar, The Kentucky Poetry Review, KOLA Magazine (in Canada), Emerge Magazine, The Journal of Blacks in Higher Education, Catalyst, the ALAN Review: Publication of the National Council of Teachers of English, Little Magazine,* and *The Griot: Journal of the Southern Conference on Afro-American Studies,* to name a few. He has published thirteen books, including nine books of poetry: *Another Black Voice: A Different Drummer* (1988), *The Beauty of Blackness* (1989), *I Fly Like a Bird* (1992), *The Whipping Song* (1993), *Vintage* (1995), *Fire Burning* (1995), *Pure Light* (1996), *Neglecting the Flowers* (1997), and *Lilacs in Spring* (1998). He has also published a book of literary criticism: *Symbolism in Herman Melville's Moby Dick* (1998). He has read his poetry at Ohio State, Williams College, Skidmore College, Norfolk State, Virginia State, the Universities of Kentucky, Tennessee, Arkansas, Illinois, Tufts, Duke, and Harvard, among others.

Currently, Slade is Professor of Africana Studies (Tenured), Professor of English, past Chair of the Department of Africana Studies at the State University of New York at Albany, and National President of The Hangston Hughes Society. A past member of the National Research Center on the Teaching of Literature, he has been the recipient of the Excellence in Teaching Award at Kentucky State University and the State University of New York, Albany, The Southern Conference on Afro-

American Studies Award, The Kentucky Humanities Grant, The Hudson Mohawk Association of Colleges and Universities Award, The Northeast Modern Language Association Fellowship, The Ford Foundation Fellowship, The U.S. Department of State Fellowship for Postdoctoral Study, and The Ragdale Artists' Fellowship, Lake Forest, Illinois. He lives with his wife and daughter in Albany, New York.